Recognize

by
Ernest Almond

Copyright © 2018 by Ernest Almond
Published by: SpitLife Publishing
Jacksonville, FL

All rights reserved. No part of this publication may be reproduced, distributed, or transmitted in any form or by any means, including photocopying, recording, or other electronic or mechanical methods, without the prior written permission of the publisher, except in the case of brief quotations embodied in critical reviews and certain other noncommercial uses permitted by copyright law.

Start Write Editors - Gerald C. Simmons & Cherie Graham
Front Cover Design - Mainland Creative
Back Cover Design - Raindrop Creative
StartWrite Project Management - Rainah Davis
Layout Design: Erica Smith

ISBN-13: 978-0-9600557-0-8

Dedication

To my wife, mother, my brothers, and sisters,
by blood, faith, and love, who continue to pray for and
support me as I pursue God's call on my life.

Also to my children, Samiyah and Ethan,
I love you and pray to faithfully show you
the way to our Father in heaven.

Table of Contents

Introduction 1

1. The Inconvenient Truth 3

2. Priority and Purpose 13

3. The Great Process 23

4. What's Missing? 35

5. Choices 45

6. God's Story 55

7. You've Got a Story to Tell 67

8. The Power is Ours 79

Introduction

There's a reason that you've picked up this book. Maybe you know me and you're just curious to see what I'm talking about here. Perhaps the title grabbed your attention, and the summary convinced you this is at least worth a browse. It doesn't really matter why you came to this book, as much as why you will finish this book. If you are like me, you have had seasons in life where you've had profound clarity and other times where you have felt like you were in a fog. In each area of life, we encounter both of those experiences and everything in between. So, right now, you are hungry for more. More clarity, more understanding, more from God.

One of the reasons we stay hungry is that we're missing out. Imagine that your mom gets inspired in the kitchen and invites everyone to the house for a Thanksgiving feast, on a random Tuesday in July. I don't know about you, but I'd make that trip, even though it's seven hours in a car for me! Imagine that you walk into the house, wanting to get a glimpse of all the glorious food you are about to inhale, and the only thing you see is the turkey. It's a large turkey, but that's it. You're going to wonder, where's the rest of the food? You know mom doesn't play in the kitchen, so, you'd want to know, where is everything you promised me?

Many of us exist just like that in the spiritual realm. We get stuck on the first thing we see. It doesn't matter that all the rest of the food has already been laid out in the next room. We'll get upset because we didn't see everything we wanted to see when we wanted to see it. We'll get mad at a situation because our perspective is wrong. That's just the world we live in.

There are things we want to see, and then there are the things that God wants us to see. Even the most faithful Christian gets it wrong sometimes. We all make mistakes, and most of us would like to do and be better. But, our starting point for changing our lives can't be the newest diet program, workout craze or new age philosophy. If we're going to be able to experience the fullness of the life God created us to experience, then there are some things we need to recognize about God, and there are some things we need to recognize about us. As you journey through this book, expect to be challenged, instructed and empowered. Most of all though, expect that reading this book will bring you a level of spiritual clarity that you've been needing.

CHAPTER 1

The Inconvenient Truth

You say, 'I am rich; I have acquired wealth and do not need a thing.' But you do not realize that you are wretched, pitiful, poor, blind and naked. I counsel you to buy from me gold refined in the fire, so you can become rich; and white clothes to wear, so you can cover your shameful nakedness; and salve to put on your eyes, so you can see (Rev. 3:17-18, New International Version).

These verses come from the prophetic book written by the Apostle John, one of Jesus' first 12 disciples. In this specific passage, Christ is speaking through John to the people of the church at Laodicea, a city in Asia Minor back in the 1st century AD. The Christians there believed their lives were great, so they treated the Lord like he was an unnecessary part of their lives. In essence, they thought their lives were cake, and they treated the Lord like He was icing on the cake! They failed to see that the truth is the reverse; the Lord is the cake, and everything else is icing. Toward the end of this passage though, the counsel is given to them that they should buy "salve to put on your eyes so you can see." God wanted them to see something that they were missing.

What is it that we need to see?

What is it that we need to recognize? The biblical text has been preserved for nearly 2,000 years. So, if these words are in the text, it is because there is a reason that we need to see. The Lord inspired John to write these letters to the churches because they each had spiritual blind spots, and the Lord desired that their vision be clear. He is speaking directly to those believers, and today's Christians share their spiritual heritage. That means there is much for us in these words also.

The first truth God wants us to recognize can be a difficult pill for us to swallow, especially in America. We don't like to see ourselves as anything other than at the top of the pyramid, but the very thing God wants us to recognize is our true condition. We've bought into our own hype for generations, because in the western world, we tend to believe we are better than we really are because we possess more wealth and resources than the people in other parts of the world do. The church at Laodicea was prosperous in the same way and Christ's message to them was "You say, 'I am rich; I have acquired wealth and do not need a thing.' But you do not realize that you are wretched, pitiful, poor, blind and naked." Ouch! That's an extremely tough word, and one that runs contrary to the way we typically think about ourselves.

If you look at all the popular books, movies and commentaries that deal with ideas of identity and self-esteem, you will see a lot of self-help, self-empowering, "you can overcome this," or "you can do anything if you put your mind to it." These are great "feel good" messages. They are both positive and encouraging. The problem is that when we buy into these books that focus on our "inner selves", auras or the universe, we're accepting ideas that disagree with what God is saying to us and about us. God loves us, but He does not want us getting full of ourselves. He wants us to be full of Him! So, when we allow our pride to boost us up to the point that we think we only need God in certain situations, we become "lukewarm" in God's sight. God sees the lukewarm person as one lacking passion for Him or conviction to live out His ways. We're not really on fire for God, and we're not really ice cold against Him, but still, God's opinion of that perspective is "I wish you were either one or the other" (Rev. 3:15)!

In this text, the Lord uses some harsh language to describe His children. After all, this is a group of believers, they are His followers and they are the church. Right? Well, the inconvenient truth is that fathers often use harsh words. Stereotypically, it is mothers who are more syrupy and sweet. They are generally the comforters when you get a boo boo and the ones who protect you from the rougher edges of life. Dads can be hard-core. If mothers are the safety net, protecting you from a crash landing, dads are the ones who will make sure you know that the safety net won't always be there. The Bible teaches in various spaces that it is a father's job to discipline his children. In other words, to prepare us for the "real" world. In the very "fatherless" society that segments of America have become, sometimes that message is far more foreign than God intended.

With that in mind, this truth that God absolutely disciplines His children, we must understand that our popular culture's representation of Jesus Christ is soft. Many times, we get this picture of Jesus that is this very meek, timid, friendly guy who wouldn't harm anyone and who wouldn't say a sharp word. Yet that is not the case at all. What He has to say, as shown in the four gospels and in the Book of Revelation, is often very blunt, straightforward and to the point. For example, a man wanted to follow Jesus, but first asked if he could stay back to bury his dying father. Jesus' response was "Let the dead bury their own dead, but you go and proclaim the kingdom of God" (Luke 9:60). After Jesus began to teach of His upcoming murder, one of His closest followers, Peter, told Jesus that it would not happen. In that moment, Jesus turned around and called Peter "Satan" because his perspective was not of God (Matt. 16:22-23). The biblical Jesus doesn't play any games and He's serious about his business. So, as we deal with some of these tough words He has to say, we must recognize that He's not communicating just to tear people down, but he's saying what He sees. He's calling a spade a spade, so to speak.

So we must set the record straight and correct our miseducation. In the Body of Christ (that is, Christians, believers, the saved), in many cases, we've been taught poorly. It's often not that our leaders wanted to mislead us. No, that's not it at all. Some of what we've been taught about our relationship with Christ is based on information that our teachers truly believed, and they felt as if they were teaching us everything that we needed to know. Often the information may even be true, but it's not been balanced. For example, when teaching

Jesus, we find that some preach God's grace, and others preach God's truth or wrath. Both are parts of God, but you can't teach the lamb without teaching the lion, right? The fact that Jesus is both grace and truth, that He's both lamb and lion, gets lost in the translation from the written word to the spoken word. Often, we are taught an "either/or" message. There are churches that seem to teach all lion, all fire, all brimstone. They teach that judgment is coming and they teach primarily from a perspective of fear of punishment and hell. There's also the extreme opposite where they are teaching all grace and love and peace and success and prosperity. In this perspective, God's love is minimized to equate to our happiness. God must "love" us so much that He wants us to be happy on our terms. Consequently, neither one of those perspectives is correct because the gospel (God's good news) needs to be balanced.

Many of us have been taught to believe that the Christian life is designed to give you comfort, ease and success. Those things can be a part of the package, but it is just like a job with benefits. You do get the vision, dental, health and retirement package, but there is something that you exchange for it. You exchange work. And no matter how much you love your job, no matter how great it is…there will be a day (occasionally) that you just can't stand it. There may be a co-worker who gets on your nerves, a boss who treats you unfairly or a manager who gives preferential treatment. No matter what your issue may be on your job, no one gets through employment with all sunshiny days. The rains will fall, even if they are few.

Unfortunately and tragically, many of us get duped. We get tricked into thinking that this "faith thing" is about us getting something from God. Then, as a result of our misinformation, there begins a series of incidents that start a chain reaction of cause and effect scenarios. The main scenario that develops is that we adopt a consumer-based Christianity. When this happens, Christianity becomes more about "what I can get from God," and not what I can bring to the table myself. Many of us treat the work of the church, the universal body of believers (i.e. all of us who believe Christ is Lord), as if it's something reserved only for paid church staff. So the responsibilities that belong to the body of Christ, you're only supposed to do if you get paid a salary. People will say:

"Oh, saving people? That's their job."

"Preaching? That's the Pastor's job."

"Evangelizing and mission work? That's their job."

The body of Christ isn't supposed to function in this way. Each believer is supposed to be all in for the mission God gave us, so we cannot continue to leave the work of the church to only the few people who end up on staff. If that limited perspective was the thought process of the early church, can you imagine how that would have affected the worldwide spread of the faith?

I believe that people only function this way because of improper teaching. I believe that when you know better, you do better. The only way that we will all "know better" is if we truly know who we are in Christ. The truth is that we were made in God's image. Since that is the case, it is important for us to truly understand who God is and just how big He is. We need to see Him properly to have a proper understanding of who we are.

So, who is God really?

God is the creator of the universe. The book of Genesis recounts the creation of our world and mankind, starting with this verse "In the beginning God created the heavens and the earth." Acknowledging that God is the source of our existence is a necessary step one in our pursuit of clarity.

God is ruler over all. Throughout the entire Bible, the point is made that "God reigns, let the nations tremble" (Ps. 99:1). God is not the servant of any nation, any political party, any social cause or any point of view. In fact, it is God who will judge the faith and works of all of us who participate in these various institutions.

God is faithful. He is loyal to those whom He claims as His own. The Bible repeats this theme throughout the Old and New Testament, and it is present in Deuteronomy 7:9, where it is stated, "he is the faithful God, keeping his covenant of love to a thousand generations of those who love him."

Isn't all this good to know? No matter what happens in the White House, you can know that "your house" is covered under the shadow of the Almighty. I know it is a cliché, but, "He's got the whole world in His hands." As a believer in Christ, God's got you covered. He has your family covered as well.

Now, if we are confident in who God is, it makes sense that we agree that He is deserving of our praise and our worship. We all should commit to be better in this area. God is not only worthy of praise and worship on Sundays or on days there are special services. He is worthy every day. Psalm 100 presents the case in this way:

> Shout for joy to the LORD, all the earth. Worship the LORD with gladness; come before him with joyful songs. Know that the LORD is God. It is he who made us, and we are his; we are his people, the sheep of his pasture (v. 1-3).

For some real world context, you should be giving Him praise in your car. You ought to be giving Him praise in your house. God should receive all the praise we can give Him, because we owe everything we have to Him. We also owe everything we are hoping and praying for to Him. He is the only one capable of answering our prayers, and He is faithful to hear the prayers of His children. So no matter what you have been worried about, you can rest well knowing that God is in control. When you cry out in prayer to Him, you never have to worry about Him missing your call. You never have to worry about your email ending up in His spam box. You never have to worry about getting sent to voicemail. He is the only one able to respond to your distress and come to your aid. He can do so using natural means or supernatural means, but the point we need to understand is that our God is so much more powerful than anything we can understand, it is pointless to try to accomplish anything without Him.

Now, as a footnote, know that it is important to understand

that even though He loves us, even though He will answer us, He does expect obedience from us. This is an important point to remember, because we are taught that God is a God of forgiveness, and He is; however, we are not always spared the consequences of every action He so graciously forgives.

We've suffered through an improper view of ourselves and an improper view of God long enough. It has hindered us long enough and blinded us to the true power at work in our lives long enough. Now that we have this information, the question is what to do with it.

Three Appropriate Responses:

1. <u>Repent from being lukewarm in your Christian walk.</u> This is the first step in the process. When I say repent, I mean: to turn away, to change your current mode of operations. This can be difficult. We get it mixed up because when we mostly think of repentance we think of an emotional display during a church service. The preacher says repent, and someone screams and then they start shouting or they run around the building. Some may even land on the floor based on what he or she may be feeling at the moment, but that is not repentance. Repentance is the simple act of turning from one direction to the other. Repenting means to turn from sin. So if our sin is being lukewarm, if our sin is not being as vigorous as the Lord would have us to be, or if our sin is not being as committed to the Lord as we should, then we need to repent. It will require us

to dedicate ourselves to the Lord on the level of commitment that He deserves. Then once that decision is made, it must be managed. You must make a conscious effort to become serious and intentional about obeying your call as a Christian, which is multifaceted. We will discuss that more in depth as we continue along in the book.

2. <u>Pursue all things that are of God with your best energy.</u> We must pursue with vigor those things that lift up God, both individually and as a church. This is a serious undertaking because it is not about just pursuing; it is about pursuing with vigor. That is very different. For a moment, think about anything in the last year or two that you've pursued with vigor. It may be an opportunity, a relationship, job search, a degree or anything else that crosses your mind. Now that you have that thing in your mind that you put real energy toward, think about that and the way you decided "I'm going all out to do this," and decide that is the same context that you will apply to your relationship with God.

3. <u>Demonstrate your gratitude to the Lord through praise and worship.</u> You may not always be able to make it to the house of God to worship. Make sure you make thanksgiving to the Lord a purposeful and meaningful part of your daily activities. Not only does it show the Lord how grateful you are to Him for all He has done, it also brings you closer to Him.

CHAPTER 2

Priority and Purpose

"Do not store up for yourselves treasures on earth, where moths and vermin destroy, and where thieves break in and steal. But store up for yourselves treasures in heaven, where moths and vermin do not destroy, and where thieves do not break in and steal. For where your treasure is, there your heart will be also" (Matt. 6:19-21).

We each value different things. Some people are fans of Nintendo, while others prefer Xbox or PlayStation. I love Android products, while my wife has Mac and Apple everything! Some people are coffee people and others are tea people. My point is that everyone has different preferences. We enjoy and experience life in unique ways. So, what may be valuable to me may not be valuable to you at all, as an idea or an item.

However, there are some things that are high in value to all of us, like time. Time is precious to everyone. It's a treasure—a nonrenewable resource. No matter what we do, we can't hold on to a single moment of time. They each pass us by with alarming consistency. The older I've gotten, the more it has seemed like time is always flying by, moving along mercilessly regardless of my desire to enjoy the perfect moment with my wife and kids or my hopes to make my vacations last one day longer. The limitation of time is what makes it so important to all of us. Time is a treasure, and how we spend our time shows where our hearts are.

The passage from the book of Matthew at the beginning of this chapter closes by stating, "where your treasure is, there your heart will be also." The "location" of our treasure, or how we spend our time, shows where our priorities are. All we need to do to figure out what is important to each of us is to map out how we spend our time during an average day or week. We may think or say that certain things are important to us, but how we spend our time shows us the truth. If what I see when looking over my daily activities reveals that I watch four hours of Netflix a day, it's fairly simple to assume that I value, or treasure, being entertained. Between all of Marvel's programming, like *Daredevil* and *Luke Cage*, movies and the thousands of other shows up there, a person could easily find himself or herself living a life in which it seems that Netflix is a priority.

Maybe it seems silly to think of personal entertainment as one of life's priorities. Still, the way we use our time shows what activities we treasure. It shows how we are willing to expend our energy, which is another precious limited resource.

Time treats each of us equally in that twenty-four hours is the same for you, me, your mama, cousin Billy, Aunt RiRi, etc. Each of us has different levels of energy, however. You may be able to function at full speed all day with only four hours of sleep, while someone else may need a full eight hours to be active throughout their day. That means we should also treasure our energy, because it too is a limited resource. All of us have things that require our energy each day, but the way we prioritize these things shows where our hearts are. In many cases, the harsh truth is that we are very self-centered or "world"-centered in the ways we use our time and energy, even if we profess with our mouths that we believe Jesus is Lord.

How can I say that?

Let's test ourselves. Let's take a step back and think about how we conduct ourselves minute-by-minute and hour-by-hour. What are we working on? What is on the agenda? If we "trade papers" and look over how we've mapped out our days, our thoughts, the problems we're trying to solve and the needs we're trying to meet, what would appear to be our priorities? What would you see when you looked at my life? What would I see when I looked at yours?

As we start to examine ourselves, especially if we are Christians, many of us will have to come to terms with the fact that we have adopted idols in our lives. We must own that there are things that we have placed as a higher priority than God in our lives. We spend hours upon hours at our jobs and then go home and continue to allow those jobs to control our thoughts and actions. We spend tens of thousands of dollars and countless hours furthering our pursuits of higher education, knowing that study after study points to formal education as the gateway to financial prosperity. So the pursuit of financial prosperity becomes king in our lives. We spend lots of money and time perfecting our physical image, buying makeup and hair and getting 'ripped' in the gym. We take supplements and record Instagram videos to show the world that we are serious about improving our physical condition. We take a lot of pride in our physical appearance. If you look at each practice, there's nothing wrong with working, educating yourself or trying to look good. The problem is that we've taken these pursuits that are good things and we've made them gods to us.

We give more attention to them than we do God.

We give priority to pursuing things that are important to us regardless of whether or not they are important to God. We prioritize our own ideas of fulfillment and then expect God to bless us like a genie would grant wishes!

Don't get me wrong. I think it's good to have a steady career. I've been blessed to work in the field of education for over fifteen years. As a childhood nerd and bookworm, I think education is extremely important for our families and communities. I'm college educated and work with teens daily to help them achieve the same. Also, as someone who has two parents (one alive, one deceased) who carried high blood pressure and Type 2 diabetes, I get the health and fitness push. I have the Beach Body workouts in the living room beside the TV right now! Having these things present in our lives is not a problem.

The problem comes when we idolize "it." When we spend our time on worldly pursuits and priorities, like more degrees, more money or six-pack abs and we neglect the things of God, we end up worshipping at the altars of the world instead of the altar of the Lord. We devote time and energy to our made-up gods while ignoring the one true God. The truth is that the fitness craze culture we live in functions just like church. Think about it. You have trainers who are teaching you the "beach body" commandments, just like pastors teach the law and love of God. The gyms are like the churches where you go and fellowship and actively participate in your fitness beliefs with other like-minded individuals. Online communities even exist for those people who prefer to work out on their own. They do not need the gym (church) or desire to see the trainer (pastor) or the other members but still want to feel as though they are connected to the community.

If we look at how we spend our time and energy, we can identify what is truly important to us. When we examine our routines or our systems, we'll see that we create ways to do what we prioritize. We find the time to do what we believe is valuable. Things that are not in our daily routines are those that are not true priorities. We may say they are important to us, just as I may say eating healthy is important to me, but if I eat McDonald's for breakfast, lunch and dinner on Monday, and Tuesday I eat Taco Bell and then on Wednesday it's Wendy's, then the routine I created does not show any evidence that my health is a priority. Recognizing this thought process, we must create routines based on what's really important.

The big-picture view of this illustration is that in order to have balanced, God-pleasing priorities, we must understand our purpose. The reason that so many of us fail to prioritize activity that is pleasing to God is that we do not look to God for our purpose or our priorities; we choose our priorities and then expect God to bless them. But that's not how God works; that's not how God works at all.

God is the source of all creation and the source of all blessing. He is the giver of all good and perfect gifts (Jm. 1:17). Who doesn't want his or her life filled with "good and perfect gifts?" Of course, we all do! However, being positioned to receive blessings from God requires that we prioritize based on the purposes of God. He made us for a reason; so while we flounder trying to find ways to fulfill ourselves through our own wits and schemes, the Lord sits, waiting for us to consult our Maker to figure out why He has made us.

Each human being who has ever lived, and ever will live, is a unique creation of the Lord. The Bible teaches early in the book of Jeremiah that before we were conceived by our parents, God already knew us, had set up plans for our lives and had given us the gifts and talents we need to accomplish those plans (1:5). In Ephesians 2:10, the Apostle Paul, the most prominent church planter of the early church, reinforces this point as he states in his letter to the Ephesian church that "we are God's handiwork, created in Christ Jesus to do good works, which God prepared in advance for us to do."

What does all this mean?

If we are believers in Christ as our Lord and Savior, the most important thing we should prioritize in our lives is our purpose from God. Fulfilling our purpose from God will require that we scrap our plans and seek His desire for our lives. We may continue along a similar path as before; however, our focus must no longer be on competing by the world's standards to be successful or feel fulfilled. We must recognize that our only path to fulfillment is that which follows the path of Christ toward the good works that He has pre-established for us. Before the foundation of the earth was laid, we were predestined to do the good works of God with our lives. So, if we've been looking for clarity on what path our lives should take or how we should spend our time and energy, we must direct ourselves to God's Word in the Bible as our starting point. It is that practice, in combination with prayer, which will lead us to live a life in which our priorities match our divine purpose.

I know. The Bible is big and intimidating, and it includes a large number of books, a whole lot of chapters and a "million" verses. Where, then, should we start our search to learn God's purposes for our lives? I'm glad you asked! I think that's a great question, and inquiring minds want to know real answers, because there is a plenty of instruction in the Bible. For this conversation, though, let's go to the book of Acts. In Acts 2, we read as the author, Luke, details the day known as Pentecost, when the Holy Spirit came down on the disciples of Christ and the Christian church was born. In one of the most famous sermons in history, the Apostle Peter lays out the case for Christ as the Messiah and then calls for all his listeners to turn away from their sin and toward Jesus. After this, Luke records the first believers' actions in response to this challenge by Peter. In these verses, we see an outline of actions that reveal God as the priority of His people and illustrate the fulfillment of our purpose.

First, we see the call from Peter for believers to be baptized. The act of submitting to baptism is a physical and spiritual activity that is an external sign of an internal change. We go down in the water to show our unity with Christ in death, and as we come up from the water it shows our unity with Christ's resurrection, testifying to all who view this rite of passage that we trust Christ as our Lord and Savior. Following this call, verses 42-47 detail the commitment the first church makes to God as their priority and the source of their purpose.

Among these, which are the purpose of the church, they demonstrate dedication to receiving teaching from their spiritual leaders, the apostles. In our cases, rather than just spending our time on social media, TV and Netflix, we should dedicate more of ourselves to the study of the Word and the teaching of our spiritual leaders, our pastors. Another purpose of the church is revealed as fellowship, which involves sharing in one another's lives, loving each other and connecting through eating with one another and consistent communication. Strong relationships are important, and in the text, the people of God recognize that their lives are more fulfilled when they have meaningful connections with each other.

Another one of the good works of believers is prayer. We tend to overlook its importance, but we are supposed to be serious about prayer, both together and as individuals. Prayer is a pathway for direct communication between a believer and

God, and the power of our prayer lives can manifest in blessing for our lives and the lives of those we care about, because we're praying for them. The Bible also teaches that the people were filled with awe and wonder because of the works done by the apostles. Now, we live in an age where skepticism reigns supreme, so we must ask ourselves, "What will it take to create awe in this generation?" The manifestation of the Holy Spirit is as real today as it was then. However, if we are not in a position to generate signs and wonders that create awe among people of the world, it remains our task to share them. We must start with the greatest miracle of all, the resurrection of Jesus Christ, and we should also not fail to share the works of wonder that God has done in our lives.

The biblical text continues by showing that the church dedicated itself to sacrificial giving; we must give a portion of what we have been blessed with to meet the needs of others: giving of our time, giving of our talents, giving of our money and giving of our resources. Christians should be the most generous of all, without expecting anything in return, because we trust God for our reward. Finally, we have a responsibility to show our sincere gratitude to a loving, unchanging God through praise and worship. Our lives will never be perfect, but they are blessed, and it is our honor to give recognition where it is due. God deserves all the glory, honor and praise for all our blessings in this life and the life to come.

The purpose of a person of God is found in prioritizing the things of God. Our greatest satisfaction will come when we recognize that our pursuits of worldly treasure will never fulfill us the way our pursuit of God's purpose will. How do we respond to this challenge of living our God's purpose?

1. Reevaluate your daily routines and look for the presence of God among them. Be sure to prioritize God's purpose and God's priority by carving out time to make sure your faith is central in your practices.

2. Seek accountability. We live in a time where people like to "do their own thing," and not really have anyone "in their business." However, if you are really going to prioritize God's purposes, you must make your faith public and create a network of accountability. Develop friendships, and follow mentors that will help you walk faithfully with Christ. This practice will not only be a blessing to you, but to your peers and to your generation as well.

CHAPTER 3

THE GREAT PROCESS

"Like newborn babies, crave pure spiritual milk, so that by it you may grow up in your salvation, now that you have tasted that the Lord is good" (1 Pet. 2:2-3).

No one starts out as a "good" Christian. How could we? We're like babies. We don't really know anything about what it means to "be" what we are; all we know is that we are ALIVE! We're excited about life and Jesus and the forgiveness of our sins and our eternal life and the Holy Spirit! We're grateful for all God has done for us, but we often don't know how to channel our energies now that we've been saved from the penalty of sin, which is death. Many of us grew up in churches or around church people, so we know what it looks like to be religious, but that does not necessarily translate into what it looks like to be saved.

I'm a perfect example. When I first responded to a call to make Jesus the Lord of my life, I was 16 years old at an evangelistic event with the family of one of my high school friends. At the end of the program, some men asked us to raise our hands, and if we did, they prayed with us, and that's all I remember. I felt "different" afterward, but I didn't know what to do. At that point in my life, my morals/fear of my father kept my outward behavior in check. So I looked like a "good person" to the people around me, anyway. The only person I told was my mother, whose response was, "I knew something was different about you." But no one told me how to do it—how to be more than just a nice guy. No one taught me how to be a Christian.

Since I had no knowledge of what to do or how to do it, my motives and my behavior regressed. I took steps backwards. To be honest, I really got worse. My lifestyle was wild, particularly in college; however, even there, the people who knew me considered me to be a "good" person. Looking back, I loved my college experience, but there was a spiritual darkness in me. Beyond the positive impact I was having in my community, college became a blend of pride, partying and sex, and I still claimed that I had a good relationship with God.

I was ignorant.

I wasn't stupid, not like what people mean when they call other people "ignorant." I was the definition of ignorant; I really didn't know what I was doing. I was just like every other person who claims Christ but never develops in those "Christ-like" beliefs. It's the same principle as some who claim they're going to get in shape, but they never learn what is required to do that. They don't learn how to plan their eating; they don't figure out how they need to exercise. They just do what feels right and think that this "hit or miss" technique should be enough. The problem with the "ignorance factor" is that ignorance trumps enthusiasm. Regardless of how excited we are about change, lack of basic knowledge is a roadblock to growth, and will prevent true success.

Getting the information you need so that you can grow starts with a choice. It's a lifestyle choice. The Apostle Peter encourages the believers of his time to "crave pure spiritual milk, so that by it you may grow up in your salvation." He's challenging believers in Christ the Lord to choose how they will fill their spirits. All of us have the opportunity to fill our spirits with teaching from the world, whether it be self-help books, college classes, talk shows or the streets. We are constantly taking in information that affects us spiritually. That information has the power to help us to be mature Christians who are sure of our purpose and position in Christ, or we can eat a diluted spiritual diet that limits our growth in our faith. To live out everything that God promised to us, we must make the choice to follow pure spiritual teachings.

The making of our "milk" choices affects our walks with God. At 16, I failed to engage the process that would help me move beyond the "spiritual infant" class; because of that, I didn't make progress. It reminds me of my toddler son. He can mimic some sound and behaviors, but he can't teach himself what he needs to learn so that he can be a healthy, smart and wise little boy. There's a process of practical learning from teachers and texts that is going to help him get there. In the same way, when someone receives Christ, the process from "baby Christian" to "mature Christian" requires a connection to good teachers and the Bible. We need to choose the best milk.

The greatest biblical teacher of all time is Jesus the Christ. His life and teachings provide us with a look at God in the purest form. The entire context of the Old Testament foreshadows His coming, and the bulk of the New Testament deals with the consequences of His arrival. However, in the four gospels, we are blessed to read of His interactions among people and His powerful teachings. It's in His teachings that we can uncover the process that will grow us from spiritual infants to the spiritual powerhouses that God always intended for His children to be. Although there are things we can do that are pleasing to God, He's not interested in our "good deeds" checklists. His teachings emphasize that our focus should be on a Godly lifestyle, not on accomplishing a set of tasks that we feel will make us look good in God's eyes. The process of living out that lifestyle choice is outlined in two texts which I believe make up the "Great Process."

We each can dig deeper into our faith through sitting at the feet of Jesus and His teachings. As we study in the book of Matthew, for example, we come across two great passages that encompass the elements of the "Great Process." These two passages reveal Christ's most basic and profound instructions, and the rest of our lives as Christians fall under these.

The first of the two great passages is the Great Commandment. The Great Commandment establishes our motives for undertaking the process in the first place. Matthew, in Chapter 22 of his gospel, records that the Pharisees (a super religious group of Jewish officials) questioned Jesus about which of the many biblical commandments is the greatest. His response:

> "...Love the Lord your God with all your heart and with all your soul and with all your mind. This is the first and greatest commandment. And the second is like it: 'Love your neighbor as yourself.' All the Law and the Prophets hang on these two commandments" (37-40).

That's a pretty big deal! Christ establishes that the most important commitment the Lord commands is that we love Him and love our neighbors. Well, what does that mean?

To love God requires daily submission of our whole selves. Our loyalty is pulled in different directions each day, and loving God is the process of redirecting ourselves in His direction. When Jesus speaks of loving God with our whole hearts, He's speaking to our feelings. The whole of our emotional being is to be devoted to the adoration of the Lord. It's from that perspective that we feel an intimacy with our Lord as we recognize how great He is. He is our Creator, our Sustainer; He sent Christ to save us from a fate worse than physical death. He provides our every need and loves us in spite of our sinful nature. He loves us even though He knows our past mistakes, and He continues to bless us, knowing that we often fall short of His standard(s). That kind of love deserves to be returned. It's with all that in mind that God commands us to love Him with all our hearts.

Loving God with our whole soul speaks to our spiritual nature. There is a part of life that is natural, and a part that many of us recognize is supernatural. In fact, we could make the case that we are fascinated with the supernatural or superhuman. Some of the most popular movies in recent times deal with superheroes, demigods, witches, aliens, ghosts, mummies, exorcisms, possessions and every other supernatural phenomenon conceivable. Thus, our interest in the supernatural is evident. If you add to that our reliance on horoscopes and our trust in fortune cookies, psychic readings, etc., then it paints a pretty clear picture that we are spiritually inclined. God's desire is that our interest in the supernatural and our interaction with it be focused on Him. We must recognize that our beliefs must point us toward the reality of the one true God, His Son Jesus Christ and the Holy Spirit, who lives within all believers.

Our minds represent our thoughts, our reasoning and our intellect. To love God with our minds requires that we study Him faithfully and continue to explore the depths of His existence. We search for understanding of the nature and character of God, and honor Him as we continuously discover His creative genius, His absolute justice and His unfailing grace. We can't really understand everything He does, but our love for Him pushes us to grow in our understanding of Him as we grow in our relationship with Him.

In the same way, our love for our neighbors, the people around us every day, should equal the measure of love we have for ourselves. Loving our neighbors as ourselves creates blessing(s) in their lives, and it has the power to show them the light of Christ through human interaction. Famous pastor Andy Stanley has been quoted as saying, "If you want to change someone, hurt them deeply or love them profoundly." We, as people of God, should be change agents in the world based on our profound love that falls in line with the Great Commandment.

How does that profound love manifest itself?

The Great Commission

The biblical text in Matthew records Jesus' interactions with His disciples between His resurrection from death and His ascension into Heaven. During that time, He prepared them for life after His final departure. Matthew 28 highlights one of these interactions between Christ and His disciples. As the chapter comes to a close, it records Jesus assigning them a set of tasks that would not only demonstrate their love of God, but also their profound love of their neighbors. It has become a rallying cry for committed Christianity throughout the centuries, and the challenge they receive here is as alive and relevant today as it was in the first century when He delivered it in person. Verses 18-20 record:

> "Then Jesus came to them and said, 'All authority in heaven and on earth has been given to me. Therefore go and make disciples of all nations, baptizing them in the name of the Father and of the Son and of the Holy Spirit, and teaching them to obey everything I have commanded you. And surely I am with you always, to the very end of the age'" (Matt.28:18-20).

If the Great Commandment is a check for our motives, then the Great Commission is a check for our methods. If we're going to be "good Christians," our love for God and our neighbors must have actions attached to them. The Great Commission provides us with instructions on which actions to take to honor the Great Commandment. When we break the text down, it actually gives us four actions, in sequence, that show our commitment to God's process of making us mature Christians who follow the lead of the Lord.

Four Steps

The first work of the Great Commission is to "go." Between Jesus' resurrection and His ascension into Heaven, the disciples continued to gather together with Christ in Jerusalem, where they were keeping a low profile, for their own safety, and being taught by the Messiah. His command to "go" signaled that their time in the shadows was coming to an end. They had received the best teaching God had to offer, and their next task was to literally go and put it to use for the glory of God. This situation resembles stereotypical American Christian habits. These stereotypical Christians go to church on Sundays and maybe even a mid-week service. Or they watch their favorite pastor on television once a week and call it church. Following that—nothing. No public practice of faith, no push to show the world around them that they love God and love people. This first element of the Great Commission shows us that receiving teaching is a great element of a vibrant faith life, but if those lessons don't "go" with us wherever we go, they are fruitless. Therefore, as we go about our life's business, we need to make sure that we are going with the purpose and presence of God on our minds.

Making disciples is what we are supposed to be doing as we go. If we love the Lord, it makes sense that we would want to share Him with others as we go. If we are Bible-believing Christians, it also makes sense that we would want those around us to develop strong relationships with God just as we are. Because people all around us are hurting and hindered as a result of not knowing the truth of God, our love for them should inspire us not only to introduce them to our God, but also to lead them down His path. Commitment to walking that path is a sign of true discipleship. We recognize that Jesus is needed in our homes, our streets, our schools, our corporations and our society as a whole. In addition, we make every effort to lead people to salvation by grace through faith in Christ, and we then must continue the process by helping them grow in their discipline as believers. Like Jesus, who started with His own people, the people of Israel, we should also start the process where we are with the people around us. We should pray to God to direct our paths as we go out into the world so that we will be confident and successful in our purpose. We must share the gospel and our testimony. We must lead others into becoming mature disciples in the faith.

One of the first steps of faith that a new believer takes is making the decision to be baptized. In the Great Commission, Jesus chooses to highlight baptism as one of the four primary acts of would-be disciples of Christ. As we go and grow disciples from every nation, we are to baptize them. But why does baptism matter? What does it mean? Baptism is ceremonial, and it is designed to show our peers and the public that we have been changed. In many ways, it serves the same purpose as a public wedding. People get married in public to declare their love and commitment for each other in front of witnesses. That public display shows the world how serious we are about binding our lives to our spouses. Just as a wedding publicly declares the union of two people through marriage, baptism publicly declares the union of a person with Christ through salvation. Christian faith is personal, but it was never designed to be private. Just as Jesus died and was resurrected in public for our salvation, our immersion in the waters of the baptismal waters shows our unity with Christ in His death. Being lifted from the water shows our unity with Christ in His resurrection. The baptism that Jesus commands, to be done in the name of the Father, Son and the Holy Spirit, places believers in the public sphere, and it positions them to continue to share their faith publicly as they continue to walk with Christ.

As disciples who love God, the last step in the Great Commission requires us to teach people how to love Jesus. Our culture has made a big deal out of learning our mate's love languages so that we can have healthier relationships. For some people, the challenge in this area is giving meaningful gifts to their spouse because that's what makes their spouse feel loved. For some, it's quality time, and others, words of affirmation. What is Jesus's love language? The answer is obedience. That's right! When Jesus is teaching His disciples about the importance of their relationship with

Him, He tells them, "If you love me, keep my commands" (John 14:15). What am I saying? The last essential element of the Commission is that we teach "them to obey everything I (Jesus) have commanded you." If we follow the Great Commandment and love God with the whole of ourselves, that kind of commitment means we willingly obey His commands. And if we love our neighbors as we love ourselves, then it should be our desire that they become disciples who also love God. As we learn to obey the Lord, we must also teach those who follow us to obey the Lord.

All of these commitments must seem very challenging, especially if you've never received teaching about the importance of living a life that demonstrates love for God. The truth is that what has been outlined in this chapter is God's ideal for believers, and He knows that, on our own, we are not capable of loving God on this level. Additionally, many of us were saved when we were younger, and we never had a thorough understanding of what God wanted from us. Well, He wants us, as His children, to be like Him, His representatives in the earth. We may look at ourselves and our failures and think that we can't accomplish the task. But we serve a God Who already knows our weaknesses and has supplied us with the Holy Spirit so that we have access to the power of God on the inside of us! That power enables us to look beyond our issues and see the God Who is the solution for them. It also helps us adopt the proper perspective and practices to bring God glory through our lives on the earth. We are able to examine ourselves and begin to live our lives in a way that honors God's Great Process.

1. Perform a love check on yourself. Do you love God with all of yourself? Are there parts of your life that you are more dedicated to than you are to the Lord? Ask God to show you yourself so that your love for Him and your love for your neighbors will be purified. Journal your thoughts as you evaluate yourself.

2. Be a disciple. Make a disciple. Check your circles, and look for God to show you someone you can help grow in faith. Don't think that you have to change this person. Change is God's responsibility. Obedience is yours. Allow God to lead you as you teach this person and others by your example and instruction how to obey what the Lord has commanded.

CHAPTER 4

What's Missing?

"You know, brothers and sisters, that our visit to you was not without results. We had previously suffered and been treated outrageously in Philippi, as you know, but with the help of our God we dared to tell you his gospel in the face of strong opposition. For the appeal we make does not spring from error or impure motives, nor are we trying to trick you. On the contrary, we speak as those approved by God to be entrusted with the gospel. We are not trying to please people but God, who tests our hearts" (1 Thess. 2:1-2).

A Mission of Faith

Love God. Love others. These two commands are the essence of biblical Christianity. As we grow in faith, living out these beliefs becomes more and more central to our lives. God's priorities become our priorities, and it shows in our practices. Although claiming to be Christian in America is less popular today than ever in the history of our nation, disciples of Christ still must recognize that God has blessed us with a unique role in the world. The world needs Jesus the Christ! Not baby Jesus from Christmas time, or the movie Jesus who looks like he's a surfer dude with a robe and a beard. The world needs the "Inconvenient Christ," who, "while we were still sinners... died for us" (Rom. 5:8)! And as those who love God and love others, it's our blessing to be able to share this Christ with the world.

Looking at the text referenced at the beginning of the chapter, you'll see the Apostle Paul explaining his work to share the gospel in Philippi. There's a strength and a passion we see him communicate as he tells of the challenges he faced, saying that they "suffered" and were "treated outrageously" there. Nevertheless, being treated badly didn't stop them from carrying out the mission to share the love of Christ. Even though their journey met with difficulty, they had confidence that they were "approved by God to be entrusted with the gospel."

It's an honor and a privilege to be entrusted with the gospel. It's been entrusted to each and every one of us who claims that Jesus Christ is our Lord and Savior. It details the most important event in human history—the coming of the Messiah! It's famously chronicled in John 3:16: "For God so loved the world that he gave his one and only Son, that whoever believes in him shall not perish but have eternal life." All the text of the Bible either points to the coming of Christ or deals with the impact of the coming of Christ. Jesus, the son of God, came in the flesh, was born through the virgin Mary, lived a sinless life in which He proclaimed the coming of God's kingdom, and His murder at the hands of the state serves as the sacrifice that paid the penalty for the sins of mankind. Because of His obedience, all humanity has the chance to be forgiven by God and adopted into His family. That's major, and that's the news that Paul and his associates were so committed to sharing. As believers today, it's just as important for us to be willing to share it as well.

My Testimony

I thank God for the people who were willing to talk to me about Jesus when I was focused on doing what I wanted to do. I walked through a phase during my teens and early twenties where I was not trying to hear about Jesus, and God was whatever I wanted Him to be. I didn't read a Bible. I didn't go to church. And I didn't think I needed either. I was content to keep living a life in which I believed that I was a "good enough" person and that being this "good person" would lead me to a satisfying life.

I thought I knew how to live my "best" life when I was in my twenties. I attended the University of North Carolina at Chapel Hill (Go Tar Heels!). While there, I made some good friends, I did pretty well in my academic pursuits and I became a "social butterfly." I was out on the yard hanging out for hours a day, I went out to the parties at the frat houses and the clubs at night, and I made time to pursue the ladies as well. I had the life! I graduated from college, got a job in the school system and continued living as I had been living in college. I felt as if I had everything I needed for the "good life." I lived in a nice apartment, I had entered a respected profession, I enjoyed the night life, and I enjoyed women! You would think that I would have been satisfied with the life that I was leading, but it was during this season that I began to become fully aware that there was still something missing from my life.

Even though my life looked good on paper and in pictures, it wasn't complete. It wasn't whole. It wasn't enough. I had a good job, but it was difficult and stressful. I was a 21-year-old man teaching high school history without any background in education. Moreover, the school that employed me had difficulties of its own, and that difficulty led to many of us working under a microscope of evaluations. I almost broke down in my first professional evaluation because my superiors seemed to go after me so hard. It made me feel like a failure, and that was the first time I had ever felt as though I just was no good at what I was doing. Part of the problem was that I still enjoyed the night life, so I was still trying to go to the clubs and the parties just like I had been doing as a college student, but that left little time for rest and really only served to feed my appetite for women. My relationships during this phase of my life were a burden of their own, because on one side, I was moving through casual relationships at a steady pace, and on the other side, I was dealing with the emotional stress of knowing that my father was slowly dying and would be gone sooner than later. I could go on, but the point is that although it seemed like I had it together from the outside perspective, there was absolutely something missing in my life.

Perceived Gaps

There's something missing in the lives of most of us – something that drives our thoughts and actions. These are our "gaps." When we think of where we are right now and then compare to where we want to be, there is a gap between our position and our desired destination. The truth is that every one of us can sit down and list the gap areas in our lives. All we need is some quiet time, pen and paper. However, for most people, the gaps we experience fall into just a few categories.

The first gap in the lives of most of us is a "Happiness" gap. As long as I can remember, happiness has been an idol of our culture. This thought process promotes the idea that we should follow our hearts and do what makes us happy. Mary J. Blige sang that "All I really want, is to be happy" while just a few years ago, Pharrell was singing "Because I'm happy!" Happiness has become something to be pursued at all costs, and even in Christian circles, you'll find that it is now more important to people to pursue happiness than wholeness or holiness. Our culture places happiness at a premium; nevertheless, anecdotal evidence and academic research show that we appear to be more stressed than ever before.

The next gap that many of us experience is a "Love" gap. We want to love and to be loved. For various reasons, we feel unloved in this culture. Perhaps we are seeking acceptance and finding it lacking. It's also completely possible that romantic love has evaded someone, or that he or she has experienced romantic love in such a disappointing or dangerous way that he or she still desperately desires the experience. On a more basic level, many of us simply want to experience the unconditional love of our parents, siblings or other relatives. We seek love in friendships, family and significant others, but in our culture, relationships are often so dysfunctional that it is difficult to find and fill one's life with healthy love.

Another gap that manifests in our lives is a "Success" gap. In our highly competitive culture, we find wins and losses in everything from social media 'likes' to getting close parking spaces! On a more serious note, we push ourselves toward an idea of what success is, and once we get there, we're often still unsatisfied. We get a promotion on the job, only to immediately begin planning our pursuit of the next promotion. We grind and grind to get to a certain amount of money, only to realize that now we want more. The success ladder carries its own pressures that, if not managed well, can lead us to an increasingly full realization that our material success is not fulfilling after all.

The last gap we will address is a "Fulfillment" gap. We like to feel important. We like to feel as if our contribution to the world around us has some significance. That desire implants in many of us a need to be the "hero" of our story. So whether we champion for the environment, justice, race relations or the poor, there is some ideal impact that we feel will bring us fulfillment in our existence. This pursuit of self-importance can be hidden behind the mask of generosity, but it's completely possible to take an unhealthy and unholy level of pride in the actions we take on the behalf of others or our causes.

We could name more gaps that exist in our lives, but the point is that there is a "here." There also is a "there." We want to be "there," but we are all stuck "here." We fantasize about what life is like over "there" – what it would be like on the other side of the gap. If I could just have someone to love me, to hold me, to be with me day after day...If I could just make a difference, if I could help save a rainforest, if I could just help one more lost cause, I would feel fulfilled. There's an illusion in which we indulge ourselves that some level of human effort or emotion can take us "there," so we'll try anything, just to fill in the gap between "here" and "there." But we'll never get there.

The Real Gap

All our human efforts to reach higher levels of enlightenment, success or satisfaction lead to unsatisfying results. More money is what we think we want, but getting it doesn't really solve our problems. We think that new relationships will fill the hole in our hearts left from previous disappointments, but these new relationships still provide limited satisfaction because people are imperfect. Whatever we believe is the missing link between us and our ideal life is a lie. The truth is that the gap which humanity so desperately needs to bridge is the "God" gap—the distance between man and God. In other words, what's missing in our lives is a REAL connection to the God of the universe.

God created man for fellowship and family. When He created mankind, He created Adam in His image and created Eve from Adam. So humankind bears the image of God. In the Genesis account of creation, it was on the sixth day that God created mankind and placed them in authority over all living beings on earth (1:26-28). When God looked at His creation,

He saw that it was "very good" (1:31). God was pleased with humanity and had given them everything they could possibly need! He also gave Adam and Eve free will, the ability to choose for themselves, and offered them a choice. "...You are free to eat from any tree in the garden; but you must not eat from the tree of the knowledge of good and evil, for when you eat from it you will certainly die" (Gen. 2:16-17). Chapter 3 records that they chose to go against God's wishes by eating from that very tree (3:6-7), and since then, the personal connection between God and man has been broken.

Because of this original sin, everything changed for us. We're not born in God's perfection; we're born into Adam's sin. So we're born disconnected from God. And we spend our lives trying to fill that void with solutions promoted by people. Eat this. Buy that. Travel there. Read that. Chant this. Go to school here. Work there. We've all been there. We've tried all of it. No matter what we try, though, we don't have the power to bridge the gap between God and us. No amount of hard work or good behavior can close the "God" gap for one simple reason—sin.

> "If we claim to be without sin, we deceive ourselves and the truth is not in us" (1 Jn. 1:8).,
>
> "for all have sinned and fall short of the glory of God" (Rom. 3:23).

The Big Question: What is sin? And if we all have it, how do we overcome it? How can we close the gap between us and our Creator?

Well, to begin, the Greek word that Bible scholars translate into "sin" actually means, "to miss the mark." What are we doing when we are sinning? We are missing the mark that God has set up for us. He's given us instructions in the Bible for how to live our lives—how to love, how to worship, how to suffer, how to pray. The way we should think and deal with every issue and person we encounter has been outlined by God (both through the Bible and the Holy Spirit), and just as God did with Adam and Eve, He gives us the choice to walk His way or our way. The truth is that every day, we miss the mark because God is perfection, and we are imperfect. Many of our decisions are selfish and short sighted. Plenty of times, we know what we should do, but we make a conscious choice to do the opposite. That's sin. That's missing the mark. And that's what creates the gap between God and the people He has created.

Those of us who know Christ as our Lord and Savior know that we can't do anything to close the gap. That's the bad news. The good news is that it hasn't been left up to us to get it done. In fact, Jesus Christ has already done all the hard work to bridge the gap! Jesus stepped down from Heaven in order to be born into a human existence as a baby to live among us. Because of that, we have a Lord and Savior who experienced the same struggles that we do. He had parents who told him what to do; he had brothers to interact with while also learning the trade of His earthly father, who was a carpenter. When He began to walk in His purpose out in the public eye, He was tested by Satan while He was weak. He was disrespected by religious leaders, and when He was falsely accused and afterward executed, His friends abandoned Him. Jesus knew hunger, He knew pain, He knew joy, but most importantly, He knew His purpose. Despite all these trials, He did what no one else could. He lived without sin!

Because Christ lived and died without sin, only His sacrifice, His effort, could pay the penalty for all our sins before God. He was resurrected with all power, and He now exists as the bridge between God and man. "If we confess our sins, he is faithful and just and will forgive us our sins and purify us from all unrighteousness" (1 Jn. 1:9). The solution to our "sin problem" and the problem of our disconnection from God is resolved by each person's recognizing and honoring whom Christ is—our personal Lord and Savior.

1. Be open and honest about the gaps you feel. It's completely natural for us to struggle when thinking about where we are vs. where we want to be. Write a list, look over it and then submit it to God in prayer.

2. Are you still trying to win God's approval? Remember that we don't have the power to please God until we recognize that Jesus is the reason we have a connection to God. Confess your sins; God will forgive you. Then walk with confidence that you are approved by God through Christ Jesus.

CHAPTER 5

Choices

"Therefore I tell you, do not worry about your life, what you will eat or drink; or about your body, what you will wear. Is not life more than food, and the body more than clothes? Look at the birds of the air; they do not sow or reap or store away in barns, and yet your heavenly Father feeds them. Are you not much more valuable than they? Can any one of you by worrying add a single hour to your life? And why do you worry about clothes? See how the flowers of the field grow. They do not labor or spin. Yet I tell you that not even Solomon in all his splendor was dressed like one of these. If that is how God clothes the grass of the field, which is here today and tomorrow is thrown into the fire, will he not much more clothe you—you of little faith? So do not worry, saying, 'What shall we eat?' or 'What shall we drink?' or 'What shall we wear?' For the pagans run after all these things, and your heavenly Father knows that you need them. But seek first his kingdom and his righteousness, and all these things will be given to you as well. Therefore do not worry about tomorrow, for tomorrow will worry about itself. Each day has enough trouble of its own" (Matt. 6:25-34).

When I was growing up, I was taught to obey...*immediately* What I mean is that there was really no room for discussion, feelings or questions when my father gave a command. He wasn't too concerned about whether I understood why he was telling me to do any particular thing. His lack of concern made life simple in a way. It was almost like, "Do or DIE!!!" If you were raised by old school parents, you know what I mean! Maybe you didn't understand your directions, and you asked a follow-up question, if you were brave. But as for me in my house where I grew up, you did what you were told without explanation, or you risked catching the belt, or the shoe, or the metal flyswatter or the...you know what I mean, right?

The passage at the beginning of this chapter comes from the most famous sermon Jesus ever preached. It's known as the "Sermon on the Mount," and in it, Christ lays down the law! It's not quite the way my parents did it, but Jesus was pretty clear in telling the people of God what was expected of them. Only unlike my dad, He actually provided some explanations to go with His instructions. For example, in the Matthew 6 part of the sermon, He's giving a warning about worry. He's plainly saying, "Do not worry." He goes a step further, however, and He gives three reasons why we shouldn't worry.

First, He says, don't worry because life is about more than what you need. We can easily get caught up focusing on what we need. Some things we really need, and some things we just feel that we need. Here, we'll call those "felt needs." For example, in 21st century America, many of us "feel" we need touchscreen technology. We are convinced that we need a phone with a touchscreen, but it doesn't just stop there. Many of us have become convinced that we "need" touchscreens in our cars, on our TVs and for our laptops. We just have a feeling that these things are needed as our lives progress. The truth is that those are felt needs; they are not essential for our survival, but we *feel* the need for them. Often, our felt needs are simply novelties or things that would make our lives more convenient. They are not necessities. What we really need to survive are food, clothing and shelter, and those are the things that Jesus is addressing here.

Even as Christ professes those three things as our needs, he still says that life is about more. He says, "I tell you, do not worry about your life, what you will eat or drink, or about your body, what you will wear. Is not life more than food, and the body more than clothes" (6:25)? The total value of our experiences in life and this body that we are given is more important than any of the material things we want to add to them. So we should not worry because life is about more than what you or I need.

Another reason He explains His command not to worry is this: God is the One Who is responsible for providing our needs. It's not about us; it's about God. He is taking responsibility for providing our every need, so we need not worry. In the text, Jesus discusses birds, grass and flowers, and He makes the point that God takes care of all of them. Thus, if He'll take care of them, we should trust Him to take care of us. Whether it be felt needs or real needs, it's God's design that as we pursue Him, He will provide for us.

The final reason Jesus gives for God's people not to worry is an image issue. He's asking us to consider the following: when we go chasing the resources this world offers, how does that make us look? We look like pagans. We look like people who have no God, and if we appear to be godless, then we simply appear to blend in with the rest of our popular culture. When we emphasize pursuit of the things this world offers, it shows the image of a God who is inadequate. To the outsider, it seems that our faith is not strong enough to provide security, to save and change lives, to heal and certainly too weak to deliver us from the valleys of life to the mountaintops.

Once again, when we focus on these things, we look like the pagans. We look like people that do not believe in God. Matthew 6:32 shares that godless people chase down their needs, but that our Heavenly Father knows that we need them. Because He knows what we need, and because we are His children, our words and actions should show a trust in our Father to fulfill our needs. We should look like the people who have hope, faith and love rather than become known for our worries. In other words, we should live a "Don't Worry, Be Happy" life! That's the choice before us.

God's Choice. Our Choice.

We must understand something. There is God's choice and our choice. God has already chosen that He will provide our needs.

Therefore, our choice, since we have a God Who is going to provide, is to seek His kingdom and His righteousness. Jesus speaks in verse 33 to the people of God and tells them to "seek first his kingdom and his righteousness and all these things will be given to you as well." This command means that if we pursue God's kingdom as our goal, we'll get food, we'll get clothing, and we'll get shelter. If we pursue God's kingdom, we'll have what we need. That's the choice we must make; God has already stated His plans to provide. We need to trust Him and do our part. And our part is to seek the kingdom. Pursue the kingdom. Chase the kingdom. That concept can be a difficult one to understand in America because our government is not a kingdom.

In fact, we struggle in our ability to understand some of the context of scripture because we don't live in a kingdom. In the most pessimistic of views, we live in an oligarchy, where a few people have power over the nation and its resources. The most optimistic view is that we live in a democracy where everyone gets a say through voting, and we all have an opportunity to participate in our own government. Wherever one falls in the spectrum, we are absolutely sure that we are not living in a nation ruled by royalty. We don't live in a place where one man's rule or what he says, is the thing that we must do, and that everyone must bow to.

Nevertheless, when we talk about a kingdom, and we are talking about seeking God's kingdom, what we are really talking about, and what Christ is really talking about is seeking to see God recognized as the only One Who deserves absolute rule of earth. That is seeking first His kingdom. It's nothing short of attempting to make God known as the dominant power of the planet. The overall intent of our words and actions must be aligned with setting up God's rule among the people. If we are believers, we are uniquely equipped to make that happen. As the body of Christ, we've been given the power and tasked with the responsibility to do just this. And so, when we talk about seeking the kingdom, we're talking about living lives that showcase God as the ruler of all.

When we make the choice to seek God's kingdom first, we must recognize that it manifests in three ways. The first way in which we seek God's kingdom is seeking Christ's absolute rule over "me." Maintaining self-control is already difficult in our culture, which urges us to be ruled by our hearts – a culture in which businesses thrive on our inability to say "no" to our own urges. It's why many of us are sick or in debt. We don't exercise self-control; we self-indulge. Regardless, the Bible teaches that one of the most important fruits to show up in the lives of believers is, you guessed it, self-control.

Furthermore, in controlling ourselves, we must do so in a way that honors our Lord, which, in essence, means our self-control must really be "Christ-control." Our choices and our actions should be ruled by Christ. There are two ways by which we submit ourselves to Christ-control in order to live the life of a kingdom seeker. First, we submit that we must know God intimately so that we may know His desires for our lives. Second, we submit that to know God intimately, we must know God's Word, and we must know God's Spirit. We must have a relationship with the Word of God; we must read and study our Bible. It is the revealed Word of God. The more we know it, the more we will know God. As believers, we must also grow a strong relationship with the Holy Spirit Who is living inside us through prayer, fasting and meditation, so that we can more clearly hear what God is saying to us in the moment. The Word of God and the Spirit of God work together to confirm God's will for our lives. If we are going to submit to Christ's rule over our lives, these two (Word and Spirit) must be allowed to regulate our thoughts, words, actions and direction.

Once we are committed to establishing Christ's absolute rule over "me," the next place we are to seek Christ's absolute rule is over our churches. We don't just seek God's kingdom alone; we also come together for the same purpose, that is the overall welfare of the church! In the same way our individual lives must be led by the Bible and the Holy Spirit, our churches must also be led the same. Too often, church is treated like a part of a weekly feel-good routine. Inside churches, we wait to be inspired by God so that we can leave church and feel better about ourselves. Church can absolutely do that, but the church experience should be so much more! Believers in Christ should come together, and as a result of our knowledge of the Bible and under the influence of the Holy Spirit, God's power should be showing up in our church experience! In God's kingdom, lives are changed, the sick are healed, souls are saved and miracles happen! Our churches should be vibrant reflections of God's promise, purpose and power to a world that is in need of all of that! However, in order for our churches to reflect that reality, we must come together to seek first the kingdom of God.

While we are seeking God's kingdom and pursuing Christ's rule in our lives and our churches, we must also consider our own spheres of influence. What that means to me is that we must seek and submit to Christ's absolute rule in our "worlds." When I consider how to handle my relationships, my finances and my career, I must refer to what I know from the Word of God and the Spirit of God. I know I'm seeking first the kingdom of God and all His righteousness when I seek God's glory beyond my own home. This means that when I deal with relationships, whether they be with friends, enemies or associates, I submit my decisions to the Lord so that my influence in these relationships promotes God's kingdom and His righteousness. When I make monetary decisions, I submit my decisions to the Lord so that their impact promotes God's kingdom and His righteousness. And as I examine my career path and the use of my talents and gifts, I submit my decisions to the Lord so that both my immediate and future pursuits place me in a position to promote God's kingdom and His righteousness. My family, friends, etc. are my world. And I want my world to recognize Jesus as Lord and God's kingdom as the most important pursuit anyone can undertake.

Kingdom Communication

In a nutshell, the focus of this moment has been to communicate that God has given us a path on which to walk, and it's up to us to recognize and follow it. Jesus taught in His Sermon on the Mount that we are not to worry; we are to seek the kingdom of God and His righteousness. The truth is that seeking the kingdom of God requires the communication of the gospel message. It requires that the gospel message be spread by me, be spread by my church and be spread to the world. It is our cross to bear. Jesus said in Matthew 16:24, "Whoever wants to be my disciple must deny themselves and take up their cross and follow me." We know what His cross was; His cross was a real and physical one. He was crucified on it, His sacrificial death paying the price for our sins. Our cross to bear as believers in Christ, is to seek the kingdom of God and His righteousness. That good work is fulfilled in part when we share good news that we have nothing to worry about. Rather, we have a kingdom to uplift, and a God who will provide for us. Literally, our cross to bear is to share the meaning and impact of the sacrificial cross that He bore for us. He's made His choice. It's time for us to evaluate ours.

1. Has worry gripped your life? Do you find yourself limited in your pursuit of the kingdom of God and His righteousness because of your fears or mistrust? Make a list of things that worry you (financial debt, career advancement, relationship, health, etc.), then pray to God to help you release your worries to Him and to help fill you with peace so that you can move past the power of fear.

2. Does Christ rule in your life, your church, the world you influence? Examine each area, and pray that God will show you in His Word and through His Spirit what you should do to reorder your priorities so that you can be a better agent, or ambassador, of the kingdom of God.

CHAPTER 6
God's Story

"As for you, you were dead in your transgressions and sins, in which you used to live when you followed the ways of this world and of the ruler of the kingdom of the air, the spirit who is now at work in those who are disobedient. All of us also lived among them at one time, gratifying the cravings of our flesh and following its desires and thoughts. Like the rest, we were by nature deserving of wrath. But because of his great love for us, God, who is rich in mercy, made us alive with Christ even when we were dead in transgressions—it is by grace you have been saved. And God raised us up with Christ and seated us with him in the heavenly realms in Christ Jesus, in order that in the coming ages he might show the incomparable riches of his grace, expressed in his kindness to us in Christ Jesus. For it is by grace you have been saved, through faith—and this is not from yourselves, it is the gift of God—not by works, so that no one can boast. For we are God's handiwork, created in Christ Jesus to do good works, which God prepared in advance for us to do" (Eph. 2:1-10).

There are varying schools of thought on what it means to be a Christian. Some interpret scripture differently, and others even disregard portions of the Bible that they dislike or fail to understand. In the same way, there are quite a few popular quotes out there about what it means to be a believer, and one that I see again and again is, "Preach the gospel at all times. When necessary, use words." People often give credit for this quote to St. Francis of Assisi, a prominent church leader from the ancient Roman Empire, but he actually never said that. That fact hasn't affected the phrase's popularity, though, and that is my main concern. On the surface, the quote seems to be a call to action for believers in Christ. However, by encouraging that actions matter more than words, this quote misleads many.

Biblical Christians are called to preach the gospel with their actions AND their words! Words are not a last resort in presenting the gospel. In fact, they are absolutely necessary in order to build up the kingdom of God, and since we're trying to live in agreement with Jesus' instructions from Matthew 6, seeking God's kingdom and His righteousness is a major priority for us all. Without the verbal proclamation of the gospel, Christianity is reduced to the same status as other world religions and even occupies the same space as secular philosophies. It becomes about self-improvement and adherence to behavior-based doctrines. Christianity just falls into line as a text-based moral code, and if people follow the code, they have the potential to receive the reward, whatever that may be. In Buddhism, the prize is achieving nirvana, in Islam it's an earned Paradise. Many faith traditions believe in a god or gods, and they promote their belief that if people work hard enough to follow the rules of their faith, then that reward is attainable.

The words of the gospel message are important because they are what separates the God message from the message of good behavior. You could take people from various religions and compare their behaviors, and those behaviors may be impressive. It's for that reason that if you compare JUST the actions of people in different religions, the truth is still hidden away. For example, what if you observe a Jehovah's Witness, a Mormon and a Christian? All you're allowed to do is observe their actions. Can you imagine with me? Each of them went to school, received an education and now have decent jobs. Each of them loves his or her friends and families and participates in community activities. You can't tell the difference yet, can you? Neither can anyone else. In fact, if you look solely at their actions, the Jehovah's Witness or the Mormon might even appear more righteous, because their religious practices produce notoriously disciplined followers.

We can also examine how those who claim each of these religions share their faith. The act of verbally sharing the message of one's faith is known as evangelism, and both Jehovah's Witnesses and Mormons are trained for it. Not only do they receive training, they even go out into neighborhoods, knocking on doors and sharing their faith from house to house. Practicing Mormons go on a two-year mission trip, once they reach adulthood, as part of the standard practice of their faith. The Christian may volunteer in soup kitchens and prison ministries, among other community services. So if you just look at each one of them living out his or her principles and you look at the Christian, the Mormon, the Jehovah's witness, how would anyone know which one faith is right or righteous unless someone says something?

Words Matter

There is a key difference that makes Christianity unique among all world belief systems, but you won't be able to catch it simply through actions. Don't get me wrong; actions are key. However, you must use words to preach the gospel. By definition, the gospel is the good news. Good news is spread by word of mouth. The gospel penetrates the heart. With God's love and power working through the Holy Spirit, the good news reveals God's will to people and provides them the opportunity to align their lives with Him. But that can't happen if we fail to share the gospel. It is practically impossible for someone to recognize who Christ is if no one speaks about who Christ is. That's why in his letter to the Romans, the Apostle Paul says how beautiful are the feet of those who preach the gospel. It's because it's the most powerful message you can share. We can feed the hungry and care for the sick, but if they never receive Christ because we failed to also use words to share the gospel with them, we have done them an eternal disservice. We will have met their temporary needs, while we also will have failed to connect them to a God Who can meet all their needs, both now and in the future. It's not enough to just care about someone's stomach or his or her shelter. We must care about the soul of each of them also.

The Kingdom's Gospel

God's people must recognize the importance of promoting God's kingdom. If we are to do that, we must love people enough to want them to be a part of that kingdom along with us. That means that if we are to love people while working to establish God's kingdom and His righteousness on earth, we must share the gospel. Why? Why is this so important? It's because the gospel is God's news flash to the world; it is the most important news in human history! No other story in human history has generated a more controversial, sustained and vibrant response than the message of Who Jesus Christ is. None! No other story has generated so much loyalty. No other story has generated so much hatred, for the gospel story is a message that affects the very nature of the human soul.

In the story of Jesus Christ rests the power of God to take territory from the kingdom of the air, which is the kingdom of the enemy, Satan. You may ask yourself, "What territory is God trying to take from Satan?" I'm not speaking of land, buildings or nations. The territory I'm talking about is the human soul, and the power to take a soul that lives in the darkness of the world and move it into the marvelous light of Christ resides in the gospel message. Certainly, we who claim Christianity as our own faith should live out our faith through our actions, but if we don't *say* anything, we can't communicate that faith. The Apostle Paul teaches that principle in Romans 10, when explaining salvation and declaring that it is not enough just to believe in Jesus. The text states in verse 10 NIV, "It is with your heart that you believe and are justified, and it is with your mouth that you profess your faith and are saved." For faith that leads a person to experience salvation, something must be spoken. And, based on my experience with the church, this principle of believers communicating faith through the gospel message has fallen to the side and, with it, the focus on seeking first the kingdom of God and His righteousness.

What is the gospel message?

"For God so loved the world that he gave his one and only Son, that whoever believes in him shall not perish but have eternal life" (Jn. 3:16).

John 3:16 is, arguably, the most famous scripture in the Bible, and there's a good reason for that. In one sentence, the Apostle John sums up the entire gospel message. Paraphrasing, he speaks to us all and shares God's good news that even though humanity's destiny is to perish, God loves us so much that He sent His son Jesus so that we wouldn't if we believe. All that is required is that we *believe. That* is the gospel message—eternal life for the imperfect person, given by a *perfect* God. We receive from God our eternal salvation by faith; it has nothing to do with how hard we work to be good people.

This idea is expanded upon throughout the Bible. For example, this chapter you are reading right now begins by quoting from Ephesians 2:1-10. This selection of text shows Paul clarifying the essence of the gospel message to the believers at Ephesus. When I review this text, I look at it as the necessary, or the essential gospel. Once we recognize the need to share the gospel, it is important that we know what we need to share. This passage provides a solid model.

The gospel is a bad news/good news proposition. The bad news deals with the condition of humanity. The good news deals with the love of God. We see the bad news explained by Paul in the Ephesians text. Paul states, "As for you, you were dead in your transgressions and sins, in which you used to live when you followed the ways of this world and of the ruler of the kingdom of the air, the spirit who is now at work in those who are disobedient. All of us also lived among them at one time, gratifying the cravings of our flesh and following its desires and thoughts. Like the rest, we were by nature deserving of wrath" (Eph. 2:1-3). John 3:16 states that Jesus came that we might not perish. The main idea that we must grasp here is that without Christ, our destiny is to perish.

Why is that the case? It is the case because, according to Paul in Ephesians, we are spiritually dead—dead in our sins and transgressions. We were born in this state. We are born sinners, who, by our human nature, miss the mark of the perfection of God. In fact, as soon as we are able to make conscious decisions as infants and toddlers, we are making bad ones! Mama says, "Don't touch that outlet." Baby boy reaches to touch it. Thus, we are established by nature as rebellious and willful beings. Now, that's the bad news. Without Christ, mankind is spiritually dead…and deserving of God's wrath. Rebellion comes with a price. When I disobeyed as a child, I would get punished. When people are convicted of breaking the law, they receive a sentence. There are consequences should we continue in the path of rebellion and sin, denying God His rightful position in our lives as Lord. Paul's thoughts in the Ephesians passage communicate that because we catered to our own desires in sin, we deserved God's wrath.

However, and this is where the good news comes in, His love for us was so great that He still chose to provide a way to spiritual life. Because of His Son, we don't have to perish! The Ephesians 2 text teaches us that God is rich in mercy. Mercy shows up when we don't receive the negative consequence that we do deserve. In His mercy, God has made us who believe alive with Christ by His grace. Grace is in force when we receive benefits we do not deserve. Even though we do not deserve God's wonderful gift because of our sin, He still has made salvation available to us as He has "seated us with him in the heavenly realms in Christ Jesus, in order that in the coming ages he might show the incomparable riches of his grace, expressed in his kindness to us in Christ Jesus" (Eph. 2:6-7). Our sins are forgiven and our souls saved by this miraculous work of God's mercy and grace!

This Ephesians 2 passage also celebrates what God has done through Christ while reminding us that salvation cannot be earned. We can't work our way to salvation. We can't do it. That's why it took such a great love to provide spiritual life for us. We can be saved through recognition of Christ's work as an expression of God's grace. "For it is by grace you have been saved, through faith—and this is not from yourselves, it is the gift of God—not by works, so that no one can boast" (v. 8-9). Why can't we boast? Why can't I boast about my being saved? I can't boast about receiving salvation in the same way that I can't boast about receiving a gift. If someone bought me a brand-new car, I could not boast that I earned it, bought it or built it, because none of that would be true. The only true boast I would have is that someone gave me this amazing gift, and I'm so happy to have received it! In the same way, the gospel message of God's love, Jesus' sacrifice and our salvation is the story of a great gift that has been given, and those of us who seek the kingdom should be happy to share this life-changing message.

How do I share the gospel?

Honestly, there's not one absolute way to share the gospel of Jesus Christ, but there are some elements of the story that are essential if we're going to communicate it authentically. Let's look at a list of them, and then we'll explain them:

> God is real.
> Mankind is lost without Him.
> Jesus is God's plan to save mankind.
> The benefits and blessing come by faith in Him.

God is REAL

To many of us, this declaration goes without saying, but we cannot assume when sharing the gospel that people are confident in the existence of God. If we're going to share the gospel, though, we have to confidently assert the realness of God Himself. God is the creator and sustainer of the universe, and He created mankind in His image, with the ability to reason, relate and choose.

Mankind is LOST without Him

The Bible teaches of the original sin of Adam and Eve, and since they disobeyed God in the garden, mankind's efforts to define its own purpose and destiny have all fallen short. We try to be what we call a "good person," but we frequently violate our own rules as to what makes one "good." We try to find fulfillment in our existence through various pursuits—love, education, adventure, wealth, relationships—but they all fail to quench the thirst for a meaningful existence. When we fail to quench our thirst for meaningful existence, we seek to numb the pain of our failure through entertainment, eating, drinking, partying, sex, gaming, etc. But nothing we can do makes us measure up, and nothing we can do protects us from that failure. In fact, everything we do to fulfill our existence outside of reliance on and relationship with God just falls into the same category of sin and emptiness that led Adam and Eve to be separated from Him. That's the bad news: because of our sin, we are separated from God. We are utterly lost without Him.

Jesus is God's plan to SAVE mankind

Sin carries a price that must be paid. Romans 6:23 proclaims that "the wages of sin is death, but the gift of God is eternal life in Christ Jesus our Lord." The consequence of sin is death, both physical and spiritual, and it cements sinful mankind's separation from God for all eternity. Jesus Christ, though, was sent to change that outcome. In life, Jesus experienced all the temptation common to man, and He was found blameless. He was tempted, but never sinned. In fact, in His innocence, He was falsely tried and crucified by Roman and Jewish officials, and His sacrifice paid the price for the sin of mankind. With His resurrection, He conquered death, hell and the grave, and before His ascension back to Heaven, He had completed His work on earth to ensure that those who believe in Him would forever more be saved from the power and penalty of sin.

The benefits and blessing come by FAITH in Him

The God of the universe sent His son Jesus Christ to sacrifice Himself, life for life, so that all who believe in Him could receive the life He came to bring. Exercising faith in Christ as Lord of our lives and Savior of our souls opens the door to a relationship with God as our Heavenly Father, and makes us coheirs with Christ. By faith, we believe and receive the benefits of salvation, which are eternal life, and also abundant life, or life to the full, as it is phrased in John 10:10. Not only does salvation bring eternal life with God, but it makes possible the full life that so many of us tried and failed to achieve on our own. Love, joy, peace and fulfillment in our being as we walk with the Lord, is the destiny for those who are saved by His mercy and grace.

Gospel-sharing Tips

It's important to be aware of each of these principles as we prepare to share the gospel, the good news, with those who have yet to receive it. It's important to have a strategy for how we plan to present the gospel in different situations, whether it be one on one with a friend or a speech in front of a crowd. It's also equally important to allow ourselves to be taught and led by the Holy Spirit so that we may be ready to take the opportunities before us to share the gospel. As believers in Christ, we have the great privilege of being adopted into the family of God! With that privilege comes the responsibility to share the truth about our Father and His desires for the people of this world and for the people in your world as well. We would do well to each examine ourselves and evaluate how well we represent our identity as children of the King.

1. Examine your words and your actions. Do they glorify God? Would they make Him happy? Would they make Him look good? It's important that our lives reflect God in a positive light to the world around us, and it starts with each of us recognizing that the power of God is to be communicated through us by our words and actions.

2. What is the gospel? Have you ever tried to present it? Find a friend in the faith, and practice with each other. Use the principles here to aid you in becoming someone who can skillfully present the gospel of Jesus Christ because in that message is the power of God for salvation of the human soul.

3. Look for resources! If you don't think you are creative enough with your words, use Google and search "how to share the gospel." There are many different strategies, including those known as the Romans Road and The Bridge, and you may find one that you feel confident in using for the benefit and blessing of those whom God sends you.

CHAPTER 7

You've Got a Story to Tell

The Gospel is the most important story in human history, and as believers in Christ, it has been life-changing for us. Because of this change, we receive the honor of sharing that message with others, hoping that they, too, will trust and receive Christ as their personal Lord and Savior. However, the gospel of Jesus Christ is not the only faith story of value that we have to share. In fact, some of the most relevant faith stories we have to share are not even included in the Bible. These stories of faith that can be used by the Holy Spirit to impact the lives of others come from you. That's right—YOU! God has shown up in your life and done some amazing things for you and around you. As a result, you have what is called a testimony. You have a story to tell about this great God! In this chapter, we are going to talk about two ways to share your personal faith.

YOUR SALVATION STORY

Once upon a time, you were not yet saved, but now you are! Congratulations! Of course, you must know the gift of salvation did not happen by magic! There is an important story surrounding your salvation, and that story needs to be shared. In 1 Peter 3:15, the apostle encourages believers to, "in your hearts revere Christ as Lord. Always be prepared to give an answer to everyone who asks you to give the reason for the hope that you have." We have hope because we are saved by the grace and mercy of the Lord our God. So the question each believer should be able to answer is, "How did you get saved?"

In explaining how to share this story, I will use the Apostle Paul's testimony, as recorded in Acts 22:1-16, as a guideline. It's in this text that Luke, the writer of Acts, records Paul's sharing of his salvation story in front of Roman soldiers who intended to arrest him and the angry mob of Jews who had just been beating him. Order is finally restored, Paul asks for an opportunity to speak. It is here that Paul shares the story of his salvation in Jesus Christ. I will break my explanation of his story into parts to clarify the elements of one's testimony of being saved.

Backstory

Who were you before you were saved? How did you define yourself before your relationship with Christ? After getting the crowd's attention, Paul, in Acts 22:3-5, begins to explain to them who he used to be. He says,

> "I am a Jew, born in Tarsus of Cilicia, but brought up in this city. I studied under Gamaliel and was thoroughly trained in the law of our ancestors. I was just as zealous for God as any of you are today. I persecuted the followers of this Way

to their death, arresting both men and women and throwing them into prison, as the high priest and all the Council can themselves testify. I even obtained letters from them to their associates in Damascus, and went there to bring these people as prisoners to Jerusalem to be punished."

We see here that Paul shares how he used to define himself; he also shares the things that used to be important to him: his status as a Jew, where he was from, what school he attended and his actions that were sinful. He frames his testimony as, "This is who I used to be and what I used to value," so the audience better understands his past prior to his encountering the power of the living God.

Becoming

What circumstances led you to profess Christianity? What led you to be born again? How did you get saved? Answering these questions requires that you reflect on the events surrounding your salvation moment– a significant part of your story. Paul, in Acts 22:6-16, details that he was on the way to Damascus when he fell blind and heard the voice of the Lord Jesus Christ. Christ questioned Paul, asking why he was persecuting Him; then, once Paul responded, Jesus gave him instructions to travel on to Damascus, where he was found by a faithful Christian named Ananias. Ananias restored Paul's sight, and then told Paul that he had been commissioned by the Lord to share what God had done. Ananias finally challenged Paul to be baptized in water and to call on the name of the Lord Jesus. In the same way that Paul explains to the crowd how he met Jesus as Lord and Savior, each of us should be able to do the same.

Bookend

How have you changed? How has your life changed since you became a follower of Jesus Christ? For any follower of Christ, there should be distinct differences between the backstory and the bookend. Salvation in Christ brings about new life, and that new life should have a new look and feel. If you were to describe an old beat down car, and then describe your brand new one, the differences would be striking. In the same way, the difference between your life before Christ and your life after Christ should be striking and noticeable. Paul was someone who prided himself on his family background and education. He was proud of his desire to do harm to Christians, also. In Acts 22, he shares that his journey began because he was leaving Jerusalem to persecute Christians, but after his salvation, he prayed to the Lord and left Jerusalem to go share the message of Christ. That's a complete turnaround, and our complete turnaround is an essential part of our story, our testimony that must be shared with others.

More than salvation

It is absolutely essential that we, as believers in Christ, share our faith testimony. Even in the case where we're not sure whether it's an appropriate time, we must allow ourselves to be led by the Holy Spirit and be willing and able to profess how God saved us. It is a life-changing message both for you and for those who will hear it from you. I have often used my various platforms to share how God saved me from my sin and myself. There were times when sharing it was a powerful experience because I knew exactly what to say. On the other hand, there have been times when I stumbled through it as if I had less than a fifth grade vocabulary. That's okay. What's important is that our faith is shared. Some people have received Christ after hearing my testimony, while other people have completely dismissed it and moved on from the conversation. It's not our responsibility to produce the results; it's only our responsibility to be faithful to use our testimony to plant the seeds.

A LIVING TESTIMONY

The story of salvation is not the only personal faith story that a believer has to share. There is a second. A believer with a growing faith, one who is open to supernatural encounters with the Lord and His power, will see God at work in his or her life, over and over. In fact, it's my prayer that everyone who reads this chapter will lead a faith life just like that—a life filled with the manifestation of God's presence, power and fulfilled promises. That's my testimony, and I want it to be yours, too! When that is your life, you have a story to tell beyond that of your salvation. You have a testimony of God's activity in your life. That story should also be shared– even if your testimony may take many different forms. God may have answered one of your prayers. God may have shown up in one of your challenging situations. He may have used people, their circumstances or even your own circumstances to communicate something specific to you, or God may have used you supernaturally so that you would be a blessing to others. The question is, "What has God done for/in/around/through you?" As a believer, you should have an answer. To help you to better understand how to frame your experiences with the Lord, I'm going to use Jesus' encounter with the woman at the well from John 4 in the New Testament.

The Usual

What's in your faith testimony? If you're telling the story, it most often begins in the realm of the mundane. In other words, our stories start off as nothing special. They may even be boring. The unnamed woman at the well that we encounter in John 4 wasn't doing anything outside what was ordinary for her. As verse seven shows, she simply came to the well to get water. It appears that she is just following through on her normal routine, nothing extraordinary, right? That's what she thought, and that's often how our stories begin, with everything going on as usual.

The Unexpected

The next part of our testimony typically occurs when something unusual happens. The flow of our day is interrupted by some encounter or circumstance that we either weren't ready for or we had not planned. That's the case here for the woman at the well. She had planned to just come to the well, draw water and return home, but verses 7-9 reveal that Jesus had other plans. He surprised her by asking her to draw Him some water, also. This request doesn't seem like a big deal, until she responds: "'You are a Jew and I am a Samaritan woman. How can you ask me for a drink?' (For Jews do not associate with Samaritans)" (v.9). Jews, at this time in history, looked at Samaritans as second-class citizens, and this bias wasn't a secret. This Samaritan woman knew that she was being addressed by someone who belonged to a people who hated her people. This knowledge interrupted her plans and drew her more deeply into an unplanned interaction with the Lord Jesus.

The Unexplainable

This piece is absolutely essential when we share our testimony. I have tried to "normalize" my testimony so that it didn't alienate my listeners, but what we must accept and understand is that when God shows up in our lives, what He does cannot be explained away by natural means. If God did it, His stamp is on it. We see that stamp of the wisdom and power of God on display as the interaction with the Samaritan woman continues. First, He takes her natural question, "How can you ask me for a drink?" and responds with a spiritual answer. "Jesus answered her, 'If you knew the gift of God and who it is that asks you for a drink, you would have asked him and he would have given you living water' (v.10 NIV)." "Living water," He says. They continue this dialogue, with His discussing the path to spiritual living water and her responses showing that she still thinks this conversation is about regular water, until she asks for it.

When she asks Jesus for the living water, this conversation takes a deep turn into the unexplainable. This deep turn is the point of no return, and after this, she begins to understand that God is really in the midst of her conversation. This is how it flows:

> "The woman said to him, 'Sir, give me this water so that I won't get thirsty and have to keep coming here to draw water.' He told her, 'Go, call your husband and come back.' 'I have no husband,' she replied. Jesus said to her, 'You are right when you say you have no husband. The fact is, you have had five husbands, and the man you now have is not your husband. What you have just said is quite true.' 'Sir,' the woman said, 'I can see that you are a prophet'" (v. 15-19).

She acknowledges here that Jesus is a prophet because He has spoken accurately about details from her life that He could not have known naturally. So not only is this Jew speaking to a lowly Samaritan, but as a man who knows that this woman has been with several husbands, is willing to speak with her about the promise of God's living water. That's the power of the Holy Spirit; that is the power of God showing up in a situation! In fact, they continue to talk until verse 26, when Jesus reveals to her that He is, in fact, the Messiah that they have been waiting for. She then leaves the well, but her water jar is still there.

The Unashamed

Boldness is key. You can't be a punk about Christ and be a powerful Christian. What I mean is that when God shows up in our lives and in our situations, we must be willing to boldly share what we have witnessed God do. That's exactly what we see with the Samaritan woman who Jesus met at the well. She left her water jar behind and returned to the town and the townspeople. When she arrived there, she didn't downplay the situation, ignore it or redirect it. She pointed her people directly to Jesus, and they responded to her testimony! In verses 29-30 NIV, we see what happened when she said to them, "'Come, see a man who told me everything I ever did. Could this be the Messiah?" They came out of the town and made their way toward him. Her testimony turned people's attention toward Jesus. The same power is present in your testimony when you share how the Lord has shown up in your life.

The Undertaking

The Lord emphasizes that we should love Him and love our neighbors. If we love our neighbors—those whom we come into contact with outside of our home—then it's our honor and pleasure to point them to the Christ Who saved our lives. It is a challenge because the message is not always welcomed, but it is God's desire for our lives because the sharing of our testimonies plants spiritual seed in the lives of others. It may spark curiosity in the lives of others, or it may blossom into full-blown faith. Regardless of the outcome, this undertaking is the path of every faithful Christian. We see the impact of the Samaritan woman's willingness to share her encounter as John 4 continues. In the text, we see that her faithfulness bears fruit—the same type of fruit that we pray is present in the life of each Christian because of the great faith of the Samaritan.

"Many of the Samaritans from that town believed in him because of the woman's testimony, 'He told me everything I ever did.' So when the Samaritans came to him, they urged him to stay with them, and he stayed two days. And because of his words many more became believers. They said to the woman, 'We no longer believe just because of what you said; now we have heard for ourselves, and we know that this man really is the Savior of the world'" (v.39-42).

If we have anything of value to communicate to our spiritually dead world, it is our testimony in Christ. Whether we relate our salvation or God's recent activity in our lives, our faithfulness to share God's glory in our lives opens up the possibility for God's glory to be manifested in the lives of others, just like what we see in the stories of Paul and the Samaritan woman.

1. Have you ever shared your salvation story? Does the thought make you nervous? I challenge you to write it out: your backstory, becoming and bookend. Then pray that God gives you the confidence to stand behind your story and that the Holy Spirit leads you into opportunities to share it.

2. What profound work has God done in your life since you became a Christian? What has He done recently in your life? Use the model presented in this chapter to present your testimony. With God, things happen in your life. Look for opportunities to share them, unfiltered and unashamed, with those around you.

3. Remember that the *results* of your sharing your faith story are not *your* responsibility. Sharing your faith story is your privilege. The fruit of someone else's life change comes by the *power of the Holy Spirit*. Trust Him, and go forth *boldly*.

CHAPTER 8

The Power is Ours

To this day, cartoons are one of my favorite forms of entertainment. I don't watch TV as much as I used to, but I still enjoy a decent diet of animation. Even as I push closer to the age of forty, I recognize that some of the thoughts and ideas that have stuck with me the most from childhood came from cartoons. Cartoons like "GI Joe" had an educational moment at the end of each episode and closed with the quote, "Knowing is half the battle." "School House Rock" interludes taught me how to use conjunctions and how a bill becomes a law. There's one cartoon, in particular, that I remember, whose message translates well on a spiritual level. I'm going to use it as a guide to help lead us to the end of this journey together.

One of the cartoons that I watched as a kid was "Captain Planet and the Planeteers," born out of 1990s America's growing interest in the effects of pollution on the environment and a desire to promote taking care of the "Mother Earth." It ran for six years, and as 90s cartoons go, it was pretty good—then. Now when I watch the intro, I can't help laughing out loud, because today it would almost certainly be seen as "corny."

Anyway, Planeteer characters were five teenagers gathered together from different parts of the world. Each had been given a ring, which possessed a specific power. One ring controlled earth, one fire, one wind, one water and one the power of heart (still don't know exactly what that one was about). Each episode, the Planeteers would be sent on a mission by Gaia, who was supposed to represent "Mother Earth," to prevent some environmental evil from happening, due to the actions of the weekly villain. Our heroic teenagers would use the powers of their rings to stop the bad guys from doing something that harmed nature or the environment, but when things became too difficult, they knew they had to unite the powers of their rings. When that time came, each Planeteer would raise a fist, point his or her ring in the air and call forth the show's titular hero. From the earth, he would fly into the air and proclaim, "By your powers combined, I am Captain Planet!" He would fight off the villain and then disappear, giving the power back to the kids. Before he restored the power to them, he would always tell them to remember, "The power is yours!"

Although this is a cartoon, it still preaches to those of us in the body of Christ. Often, we look for spiritual heroes to do the work that God assigned to the whole body of Christ. We look for the pastors and missionaries, the televangelists and the Christian celebrities to do the work of building up God's kingdom, while most of us prefer to sit back and enjoy the benefits and blessings of the kingdom without putting in any work. Jesus teaches, "Seek first," but too often, we believers take a "wait and see" approach to kingdom pursuits. We wait until the "hero" has shown up, and then we may join in the action.

That's quite the passive spiritual existence, and not what God intended for your life as a Christian. That's not what God intended for the average small church on the corner in the neighborhood. Jesus ascended into Heaven to be seated at the right hand of God, and Holy Spirit came down to inhabit every believer. Holy Spirit is the person of God and the power of God living on the inside of each of us. That means, to take from the Captain Planet cartoon, that rather than sitting back and waiting on spiritual heroes, we should recognize that the power is ours! God has given us everything we need to live the life that He's designed for us. He promised in Matthew 6:33 that those who seek the kingdom and His righteousness would have their material needs met. The Bible itself provides the revelation of Who God is and how He desires to interact with humanity. Ephesians 6 describes the armor of God that is available to each believer for the purposes of spiritual warfare. In Chapter 5 of Paul's letter to the Galatians, he lists how the fruit of the Holy Spirit manifests in our lives: love, joy, peace, forbearance, kindness, goodness, faithfulness, gentleness and self-control. God has given us everything we need to be kingdom builders for His glory. God has added everything necessary to you and at the same time taken away every excuse.

The Power of the Church

The universal church consists of every single person who professes Jesus Christ as Lord and Savior. If that's you, then you are part of what's called the "body of Christ." We are the body of Christ because together we are supposed to function in the same way He did on the earth. We are to be His ambassadors, communicating His message, and His servants, doing His earthly work, until He returns. So all that He demonstrated in teaching the Word of God and living the Way of God was done to prepare us for our purpose and privilege, which now belong to us through the indwelling power of the Holy Spirit. Jesus is recorded as telling His disciples, "Very truly I tell you, whoever believes in me will do the works I have been doing, and they will do even greater things than these, because I am going to the Father" (Jn. 14:12). Please take note here that Jesus is not singling out any faith "heroes." He doesn't say whoever is my *apostle* or my *prophet* will do the works I have been doing. He specifically says, "*Whoever* believes in me." Therefore, Mr. or Ms. Christian, if you believe Jesus at His word, then you, too, must believe that the power and responsibility of building up the kingdom of God is yours. You have the Word of God, you have the Spirit of God, and as we continue to discuss this, it is just as important that we recognize that we also have each other–the church.

Church Folks

Because many of us have experienced hurt, betrayal or hypocrisy in our church experience, we don't dedicate ourselves to God and His purpose for our lives as we should. We neglect the Word, we quiet the voice of the Spirit, and we disengage from the local church. Then we claim that it's okay to function in this way as spiritual independent agents because You are free to eat from any tree in the garden As a Christian, you are a part of the body of Christ. What that means is that every other true believer on Earth is also your brother and your sister. The Lord instructs us that we can't claim to love Christ and reject His body. In fact, any attempt to do so weakens both your individual walk with Christ and the local church's ability to represent Him. What the Bible actually teaches is that the relationship between believers is more important than the relationship between family members. As Jesus taught a crowd of people, his family sent a message that they were outside and wanted to talk to Him. "Jesus replied, "Who is my mother, and who are my brothers?" Pointing to His disciples, He said, "Here are my mother and my brothers. For whoever does the will of my Father in heaven is my brother and sister and mother" (Matt. 12:48-50). The Bible also teaches in Galatians 6:2 that to bear each other's burdens fulfills the law of Christ, and Jesus states in John 13:35 that people will be able to identify His disciples because of their love for each other. The body of Christ, and thus the local church, is designed to function in a way that shows the genuine and meaningful connection of believers to each other.

It is God's desire for His children, those of us who are saved, to be sincere in our relationship with Him and in our relationship with each other. The collective known as the local church represents God's design to help us live our faith lives in fullness. The original Christian church described by Luke in Acts 2 reveals what God had in mind:

> "They devoted themselves to the apostles' teaching and to fellowship, to the breaking of bread and to prayer. Everyone was filled with awe at the many wonders and signs performed by the apostles. All the believers were together

and had everything in common. They sold property and possessions to give to anyone who had need. Every day they continued to meet together in the temple courts. They broke bread in their homes and ate together with glad and sincere hearts, praising God and enjoying the favor of all the people. And the Lord added to their number daily those who were being saved" (Acts 2:42-47).

When God designed the church, He desired that we come together to receive divine teaching and see signs and wonders from our spiritual leaders. In addition, God desired that we connect with each other, person to person and life on life, that we meet in each other's homes breaking bread and praying together. God's church was designed for us to serve, making sure we took care of the needs of the people, even when it required personal sacrifice. God's church was designed to share love, the Word and the faith, praising God and leading others in engaged community so that the church would continue to grow because of new people "who were being saved." The Acts 2 text presents a beautiful picture of what it looks like for people to seek first the kingdom of God and His righteousness, with the promise that all our needs will be provided for us.

God wants us to know and understand that the people of the church are never going to be perfect, but the *purpose* of the church is *perfect*. In God's design, the church is designed so that the local church experience is both a place where the believer is *blessed* and a place where the believer is a *blessing* to others. Any thoughts of a Christian faith that are not centered on loving God, loving others and pursuing the establishment of the kingdom of God are not authentic in the eyes of the Lord. There is a power He has, and there is a power He has given, and because of it, when it comes to kingdom building on earth, the power is YOURS! Really, as the body of Christ, the power is OURS.

You need the local church. The local church needs you. God intends to use the local church today in the same way He used the local church in Acts 2. The local church, through the teaching of the Word and demonstration of God's power, strengthens believers in their most holy faith. The people of the local church work together to share the gospel of Jesus Christ so that more and more people can join us in the family of God. And the local church changes lives through its service to mankind. Local churches come together to feed the hungry, provide clothes for those in need and shelter for the homeless. Programs that aid in recovery from addiction, in obtaining financial health, in bringing joy to children and the elderly are all undertaken by the local church. Between doing the spiritual work of allowing God's presence and power affect the nature of people's reality, and doing the practical work of providing for people's needs, the local church provides opportunity for each individual Christian to be actively engaged in the mission left behind for the body of Christ.

The truth is this: The church is made up of the people of God, including you. The church has been given the power of God through the Holy Spirit in order to promote Christ IN the world. The same Holy Spirit-power and the same love that was so dynamically present in the Acts 2 church is available to every believer and every church today. Just as then, salvation in Christ should be a life-altering event for us, and our dedication to seeing God's kingdom built up through our lives and work as the church should be evident in our daily lives. Your life and my life have been changed forever by the love of God, and praise be to God for giving us the power to effect this change in the lives of others. Now *this* empowerment should be something to shout about!

1. Are you a "solo" Christian? Are you disconnected from God's church, and thus, your spiritual family? I challenge you to find a biblically sound church, not just to attend, but to join with them in fulfilling the call and challenge from Christ to "seek first the kingdom of God."

2. Perhaps you still have a "beef" with someone from your past church experience, which has kept you from going back to a local church. In God's love, forgive that person for hurting you, and make a move past the hurt by refusing to be held hostage by the pain that he or she has caused you.

3. Accept the reality that God's love for you has come with a price. He expects a real relationship with you. He expects a relationship in which you prioritize Him in your life and promote Him in the lives of others you encounter. This mission may seem like a burden if you've never wholly dedicated yourself to pleasing God in your Christian walk. God loves you so much that He has given you access to every spiritual tool you

will need along the way to fulfill the purpose for which He made you and has REDEEMED you. Go forth, and prosper!

www.ingramcontent.com/pod-product-compliance
Lightning Source LLC
Chambersburg PA
CBHW050604300426
44112CB00013B/2067